Stay In Your Blessed Place

Tracey K. George

DEDICATION

For everyone that dares to enter and remain in *The Blessed Place*

CONTENTS

ACKNOWLEDGMENTS

Thank you for all your prayers and support

Introduction

As I preached this sermon years ago, I struggled with the content. God told me that I was missing the point. Seriously; I did not understand what God was talking about. Stay in Your Blessed Place... what was that? I didn't have a clue. In other words, I had to live it first before I could share it with you. So now you've had your Calgon moment... You've taken a few days off to get your mind together. You feel like you are on top of the world. Everything sounds great. Unfortunately, time has passed and you find yourself back at the same spot you were in before. Something happened that threw you off your game and you've begun to question everything.

Time to take inventory. You've stepped up in your prayer time with God. Check! You've spent more time meditating on His Words. Check! Now what? You still don't get it; something is missing. Why are you feeling as if you have returned to square one? What is going on? So many questions...

Let me interject right here an important clue to the solutions you seek. You have learned about The Blessed Place; however, you haven't quite figured out how to maintain your position there. Having the information is great; however, knowing how to use it is even better!

With that being said... Welcome! Welcome to the possibility to *Stay In Your Blessed Place*. Why did I say possibility? It alludes to the fact that you are supposed to live your life as God designed it to be; however, it's totally up to you. That's right! You must embrace the fact that it is possible to do and desire to live it now! Which means, you have more work to do. Don't feel bad... This is the journey. As we continue to live, the Lord made sure we would have help to guide us along the way.

Hence the reason the third Book in The Blessed Place Series was written; it gives you tips and guidelines to assist you with staying in your place. As we dive into the Word together, you will see the Word of God guiding you through your process as it leads you to the answers you've been seeking for so long.

Know the Truth

"And ye shall know the truth, and the truth shall make you free."
John 8:32 KJV

When you think of the truth what comes to mind? When I was little, my mom looked in the cookie jar and discovered that a few cookies were missing. "Who took the cookie out of the jar", she said. I replied, "Not me" knowing fully well I took the cookie. I also remember a time when I called out from drill (military); I told them I was "sick" when actually I didn't feel like going in… Oh yeah, that was me. Boy oh boy….. During my younger days, I had a weird relationship with "the truth". Some of my encounters were welcomed while others were rejected. Sometimes I simply felt that "the truth" didn't like me. Regardless of my feelings, I continued to pursue it. I had a desire to learn. This desire led me to books, the Bible, and asking numerous questions. I sought it ought…. Throughout this time of growth, I discovered that God desires the truth from us though we have often eluded to that fact.

Psalms 51:6 KJV
"Behold, thou desirest truth in the inward parts: and in the hidden part thou shalt make me to know wisdom."

Notice it said that He desires the truth in the inward parts… this means you have to let go of the masks you've been wearing for far too long.

That masks hides you and keeps you from really connecting to anything or anyone. As long as you wear it no one gets to see the real you.

Even so, the Scripture tells us that the truth will make us free. So how do we go from being bound without it to a place of freedom? It requires the truth.

Psalm 15:2 MSG
"Walk straight, act right, tell the truth."

"For God's Word is solid to the core; everything he makes is sound inside and out. Now we must take into consideration that knowledge of the truth requires more than cognizance (just being aware of it); it requires intimacy (close familiarity or friendship). You must develop an affinity for the truth which doesn't happen overnight; it is developed over time.

Knowing the truth will shine the light causing the arrow to release in the direction of Your Blessed Place. God's Word is crystal clear. All it takes is an understanding of what He wants concerning you and your life and then walk it out. Walking in the truth requires His guidance. He knows what we have need of and how to bring it to pass. We must pay attention to His will and implement His word in every aspect of it. Allowing His Word to shine in our dark places will give us the needed instruction which will enhance our walk.

Psalms 119:105 KJV
Thy word is a lamp unto my feet, and a light unto my path."

Bullseye! Can you see it? *Stay in Your Blessed Place* requires the Word of God! How often do you read it? How often do you meditate in it?

Psalms 1:2 KJV
"But his delight is in the law of the Lord; and in his law doth he meditate day and night."

If you are going to excel in your walk, you must have His word as your main source. It must become your daily bread and your guiding light. Let me give you an example found in the Word of God…

2 Samuel 12:1-7 KJV
"And the Lord sent Nathan unto David. And he came unto him, and said unto him, There were two men in one city; the one rich, and the other poor. The rich man had exceeding many flocks and herds: But the poor man had nothing, save one little ewe lamb, which he had bought and nourished up: and it grew up together with him, and with his children; it did eat of his own meat, and drank of his own cup, and lay in his bosom, and was unto him as a daughter. And there came a traveller unto the rich man, and he spared to take of his own flock and of his own herd, to dress for the wayfaring man that was come unto him; but took the poor man's lamb, and dressed it for the man that was come to him. And David's anger was greatly kindled against the man; and he said to Nathan, As the Lord liveth, the man that hath done this thing shall surely die: And he shall restore the lamb fourfold, because he did this thing, and because he had no pity. And Nathan said to David, Thou art the man. Thus saith the Lord God of Israel, I anointed thee king over Israel, and I delivered thee out of the hand of Saul;"

At first glance, you understand why David is prepared to use his kingship to deal with this injustice. How could this rich man take advantage of someone less fortunate? However, Nathan brings up an interesting point. He introduces a curve ball...The truth has been revealed. David is the rich man in the story. So now what?

You must admit that there are many in the Church with that type of mentality. This is the reason why the Father warns us that many in the Church will not be saved. People don't want to address it because they would rather pretend that the skeletons are not in the closets. As a child of God, it is our assignment to make sure that we tell the totality of what He has told us to the people regardless of their connection to us. Even if it means a shift in the relationship you have with them. Jesus loves us so much that He told us the Truth.

Listen Up

"If only you will listen to and obey the voice of the LORD your God, to observe carefully all these commandments which I am commanding you today."
Deuteronomy 15:5 AMP

Growing up under my mother's watchful eye kept me covered until I came into awareness of God for myself. When I was a young child, I would go to my mom and ask, "Mom what is God saying?" and she would say "go ask Him." I thought, "Mom is being mean, she heard God why can't she tell me." The Lord said to me one day, "No she is not being mean, she is training you so that you can listen to me for yourself." God wanted me to be trained to pay attention to Him. How amazing! Years later, when the time came, I told my kids the same thing. During my early years, I learned how to listen and obey the Lord which became two invaluable lessons that proved to be needful throughout my journey in life to this very day.

Exodus 23:22 AMPC
"But if you will indeed listen to and obey His voice and all that I speak, then I will be an enemy to your enemies and an adversary to your adversaries."

When you truly begin to listen and respond with action then nothing will be withheld from you. In fact, He will be an enemy to your enemies. Who will be able to stand against you? The Word of God is clear, you must listen and obey.

He desires to speak with us as we journey through this life. Tuning in to His voice affords you the opportunity to connect with God on another level. One example of this is seen in the relationship between Moses and our Father. It began with God's voice…

Exodus 3:1-4 NLT
"One day Moses was tending the flock of his father-in-law, Jethro, the priest of Midian. He led the flock far into the wilderness and came to Sinai, the mountain of God. There the angel of the Lord appeared to him in a blazing fire from the middle of a bush. Moses stared in amazement. Though the bush was engulfed in flames, it didn't burn up. "This is amazing," Moses said to himself. "Why isn't that bush burning up? I must go see it." When the Lord saw Moses coming to take a closer look, God called to him from the middle of the bush, "Moses! Moses!" "Here I am!" Moses replied."

As you read this particular passage, you see that Moses was working. He had no idea that God was getting ready to call his name. Yet, he wasn't sitting around. Moses was tending the animals of his father-in-law and led them out into the wilderness. Then he came to Sinai, the Mountain of God.

Do you see it? Moses was working and had no idea that God was leading him to Himself. Once there, he noticed something. Away from the family, he was able to see. He decided to go take a closer look at the burning bush. Now notice what happened when Moses decided to move CLOSER; the Lord took NOTICE. Yes! When Moses moved the Lord saw and responded by calling Moses' name. Many believe going through the motions will garner the same results. Not true! You have to get up from the spot you are in and move nearer to God.

Develop your relationship with Him before long the desire to run your own life will subside. Instead, you will learn that God is willing and ready to guide your life; He will direct your path. Before you know it, the journey will become a no-brainer. That doesn't mean it will be a cake walk; however, you will learn that you are not alone. God is with you every step of the way.

Psalms 48:14 KJV
"For this God is our God for ever and ever: he will be our guide even unto death."

Oftentimes, I hear some say that they are struggling with this. They can't relate this scripture to anything in particular. Yes some have no idea what it feels like to be fathered. So this may seem a bit foreign. Learning to rely on God takes faith. The reason it appears that the struggle continues could be that you have not released the controls. Let's be honest learning to trust God takes time especially when you've been doing your own thing all this time.

Proverbs 3:5-12 MSG
"Trust GOD from the bottom of your heart; don't try to figure out everything on your own. Listen for GOD's voice in everything you do, everywhere you go; he's the one who will keep you on track. Don't assume that you know it all. Run to GOD! Run from evil! Your body will glow with health, your very bones will vibrate with life! Honor GOD with everything you own; give him the first and the best. Your barns will burst, your wine vats will brim over. But don't, dear friend, resent GOD's discipline; don't sulk under his loving correction. It's the child he loves that GOD corrects; a father's delight is behind all this."

Did you take note of the part that said listen for God's voice in everything you do? Everything you do... that takes real concentration from us. He wants us to pay attention to more than the words. We must focus then we can follow through with the task at hand. He tells us to RUN to HIM! Take the time to do that right now! RUN to HIM!!

Ways of Life

"Thou hast made known to me the ways of life; thou shalt make me full of joy
with thy countenance."
Acts 2:28 KJV

In this season, God reminded me that you have to know where your
Blessed Place is. You have to connect to it until you're tangled in it; it's
like a vine wrapped around you. You would have to cut all of it away to
attempt to sever the ties. You have to get connected to your blessed
place like that.

John 15:4-5 AMPC
"Dwell in Me, and I will dwell in you. [Live in Me, and I will live in you.] Just as
no branch can bear fruit of itself without abiding in (being vitally united to) the
vine, neither can you bear fruit unless you abide in Me. I am the Vine; you are
the branches. Whoever lives in Me and I in him bears much (abundant) fruit.
However, apart from Me [cut off from vital union with Me] you can do nothing."

The Word says you cannot bear fruit unless you abide in Him, The true
vine. Apart from Him you cannot do anything. The blessed place
should be a way of life for us not a temporary spot. In fact, it should be
something occupied and maintained. In other words how have you
been living?

9

Does your life reflect what God has spoken to us through His Word? Too many relationships, families, ministries, businesses, etc.... have been destroyed because someone failed to understand this point. Pride can kill! One of the things you must consider in this life is that there is more to *The Blessed Place* than meets the eye; it involves life changes.

We must be willing to submit ourselves to Him so we will know His will for our lives..... The place He ordained for us. This place is the "blessed" place. It is a place set aside for a specific function, people, and/or time. So often we fail to admit to ourselves that we haven't taken the time to consider that God really does order our steps..... Is it possible we didn't know it?

He wants His house to maintain the order that He had already set the standard for. He is the Word, and from the beginning He has been telling people this is the way He wants it. Unfortunately, folks have been running His ship the way they want to run it. So what happens is you have folks doing things their way. Now, the rest of the world is saying we're going to join in too.

Now, the enemy laughs and the church has picked up a reputation of being fake, phony and foolish. Even the media comes forward to talk about the leaders. Thank the Lord for the ones that reflect the image God intended. Then they post the pictures of all those who were supposed to be representatives of Christ and have failed. When the Bible says men would see our good works and glorify the Father...

Matthew 5:16 KJV
"Let your light so shine before men, that they may see your good works, and glorify your Father which is in heaven."

The Bible says we are supposed to be the epistles read by men. This means someone is always watching.

2 Corinthians 3:2-3 HCSB
"You yourselves are our letter, written on our hearts, recognized and read by everyone. It is clear that you are Christ's letter, produced by us, not written with ink but with the Spirit of the living God — not on stone tablets but on tablets that are hearts of flesh."

From the moment we say that we belong to God, many will watch to see the reflection of God in us. Hence the reason some have no respect for those that say they are Christian especially at a time where many call themselves but the reflection of God isn't visible. According to the Word of God we are supposed to be a real reflection of Him. When you look in the word what do you see? Do you reflect what the word says? Unfortunately, when I look among some of my Christian brothers and sisters; the sight saddens me. Instead of making the necessary changes some begin to use excuses...

It has become easy to use excuses such as "I'm only human". Has falling and failure become a way of life or have we learned to accept mediocrity? We must consider the alarming fact that continuing to make excuses causes one to believe that the standard that God set is impossible for anyone to achieve. At some point, we began to measure ourselves by other people and based on the outcome we decide whether we are on point or not. In actuality, we have set ourselves up to lower our standards so that we don't expect much from our own lives. Staying on course reminds us that there is a goal and I'm not out here just aimlessly wandering around with no focus or direction.

1 John 2:28 MSG
"And now, children, stay with Christ. Live deeply in Christ. Then we'll be ready for him when he appears, ready to receive him with open arms, with no cause for red-faced guilt or lame excuses when he arrives."

Stay with the Anointed One and live deeply in Him. Keep in mind this process takes time. God gives us instructions to follow; failure to follow them can adversely hamper or prohibit our ability to remain. So we must allow change to occur..... God trims/prunes us so we can produce more fruit and remain connected to the True Vine!

John   15:1-2   HCSB
"I am the true vine, and My Father is the vineyard keeper. Every branch in Me that does not produce fruit He removes, and He prunes every branch that produces fruit so that it will produce more fruit."

The Word says that every branch that does not produce fruit He removes. At some point, you must ask yourself is this a way of life for me or am I looking for a quick fix? Do you run to church with the hope that someone will prophesy to you and tell you everything is going to be alright?" When are we going to learn that God wants us to grow up? He wants us in the blessed place... the place He has designed just for us.

This is supposed to be the way of life. You are supposed to be in His Word constantly. That same word teaches you. The Word is supposed to find us and when it does we are supposed to do the work to get in place.

Psalms   1:2   KJV
"But his delight is in the law of the Lord; and in his law doth he meditate day and night."

He also said Line upon line, precept upon precept (Isaiah 28:10). He desires for you to follow His word. No one should be expected to eat the entire Word in one setting and attempt to do everything you've just read. Impossible! You have to take a little bit at a time. This is what He has told us otherwise the wild beast (Satan) will come in and you will not be able to deal with him. God wants you to be able to win and He has set it up where you will be able to win every time. However, you have to be honest with yourself. You have to be truthful with yourself. You have to admit your faults.

When He expose your weakness you don't sit there trying to look around and see who saw you; no you have to admit it. If they would have done their first work behind closed doors (repenting, praying and reading the word) when the Father first showed it to them, it would have remained between them and God. And may be the few that saw them. The Father would have sent someone your way that could minister to you privately straight from the word of God to get you back on track; to the way of life. No one is exempt from God's Word. It is time to face the fact that you must stay on the potter's wheel. This is supposed to be a way of life.

Psalms 15:1-5 KJV

"Lord, who shall abide in thy tabernacle? who shall dwell in thy holy hill? He that walketh uprightly, and worketh righteousness, and speaketh the truth in his heart. He that backbiteth not with his tongue, nor doeth evil to his neighbour, nor taketh up a reproach against his neighbour. In whose eyes a vile person is contemned; but he honoureth them that fear the Lord. He that sweareth to his own hurt, and changeth not. He that putteth not out his money to usury, nor taketh reward against the innocent. He that doeth these things shall never be moved."

In Psalms, it asks the question who shall dwell in His Holy hill. Then He begins to give you a list of things that will qualify a person to enter in. He did not say only to those who go to church on Sunday or those who choose to open their Bibles from time to time. He said anyone who hears His words. What does that mean? It means if you hear My Words, no matter how it is packaged; whether you are saved or not. If you just so happen to pass a billboard and saw His Word written on the billboard; it is still any man who hears My Words. So many people have limited the ability of God's Word to advance and to come forth so that anyone can hear it. It is not only Christians He is talking about. He said anyone who hears My word and makes a choice not to obey it.

13

John 12:44-48 KJV
"Jesus cried and said, He that believeth on me, believeth not on me, but on him
that sent me. And he that seeth me seeth him that sent me. I am come a light
into the world, that whosoever believeth on me should not abide in darkness.
And if any man hear my words, and believe not, I judge him not: for I came
not to judge the world, but to save the world. He that rejecteth me, and
receiveth not my words, hath one that judgeth him: the word that I have
spoken, the same shall judge him in the last day."

Now, here comes the part that got me. He said, "I do not judge." Now, many folks walk by that and think the Lord doesn't judge me. They may say, I am just human and He loves me. They make those excuses without understanding what He just actually said. He wants to save you but it's up to you. Catch that nugget right there… He chastens those He loves. So is the Blessed Place the place that you are trying to achieve or is the Blessed Place. Jesus is saying, if you have heard My Words and you refuse to obey what I am telling you; then I
have already counted you as a part of the world and not of
Me. The Bible tells you that God is going to judge the world.
What Jesus is saying here is, in the flesh I will not judge you. I'm here on the assignment to save you. So, if I'm here to save you, how can I judge you as well? I'm just going to do My assignment and save the world; that is all. So now we must consider the love factor. We declare our undying love for Jesus yet He was crystal clear...

John 14:15 AMPC
"If you [really] love Me, you will keep (obey) My commands."

Jesus said to Peter, "Love thou me?" Peter responds, "Yes Lord, I love you." Jesus asked him two more times, because if he loved Him he would obey. Nobody is going to have to tell him to keep them. If you already love Him it is a given that you will obey Him. Your obedience is the proof that you do love Him. Proof is not telling God every morning that you love Him. Constantly telling God, "I love you Lord" proves nothing if there is no obedience.. A lot of people wait for somebody to come and tell them, will you please do so and so. When you love God, you love him so much that you do not have to be told over and over again to do stuff for Him.

So this leads to people thinking they are in the Blessed Place but are actually walking alongside it. The Blessed Place is not occupied by many people. This is why the Word says that the gate is narrow, and broad is the way to destruction.

Matthew 7:13-14 AMPC
"Enter through the narrow gate; for wide is the gate and spacious and broad is the way that leads away to destruction, and many are those who are entering through it. But the gate is narrow (contracted by pressure) and the way is straitened and compressed that leads away to life, and few are those who find it.

There are so many people near the way but only a few have actually gotten on the path. The Word tells us if the righteous are scarcely saved then what will happen to everybody else. I say to you read the fine print. It is right there staring back at you. Do not miss your moment with the Father by listening to all the broad talk that you miss the fine print.

Where Do You Stand?

"And if the righteous scarcely be saved, where shall the ungodly and the sinner appear?"
1 Peter 4:18 KJV

When Jesus chose his disciples, He knew once He began to work with them; they would come on through. It took Peter a little while but eventually, he got it.

When we consider the "righteous" what comes to mind? The Word says, "If the righteous scarcely be saved"... So those considered to be in right standing, if they scarcely be saved, where will the rest appear? Hmmm.... That sounds like slim pickings to me. That means many should not be walking around with their chest stuck out and their head held up like they are really the righteous. This brings to the forefront the difference between those that follow Jesus and His teachings versus The Pharisees and Scribes. There's more to knowing where you stand in God then going to church, quoting scriptures, and looking the part.

1 Peter 4:16-19 KJV
"Yet if any man suffer as a Christian, let him not be ashamed; but let him glorify God on this behalf. For the time is come that judgment must begin at the house of God: and if it first begin at us, what shall the end be of them that obey not the gospel of God? And if the righteous scarcely be saved, where shall the ungodly and the sinner appear? Wherefore let them that suffer according to the will of God commit the keeping of their souls to him in well doing, as unto a faithful Creator."

Do you realize that God is specific in what He wants from us, His people? If you read the first verse from the same chapter (1 Peter 4), you will see that Christ suffered and we are supposed to arm ourselves likewise,

"Forasmuch then as Christ hath suffered for us in the flesh, arm yourselves likewise with the same mind: for he that hath suffered in the flesh hath ceased from sin;

Armed with having the same mind concerning suffering, continue reading 1Peter 4 and you will see what He considers suffering. The masks worn for cover give off the wrong idea of this passage exposing a false impression of one's position. In other words, it can make you believe yourself to be something you are not. So my question to you is simple… After everything you've been through have you ever stopped to think about where you stand with God? Could your position be based on what you've heard someone say but never studied it for yourself? Taking on the mind set of someone else you believe to be righteous knowing fully well that their stance is the opposite of what God wants for His people is dangerous. Some have taken the scriptures and flipped them to fit what they want so much until they don't have a clue what God actually wants.

You can quote the scriptures and do all of this; but if God is not found in you then you are not His. Many will say well, you can't see my heart. Well, from the heart, the mouth speaks. What we see reflected is the result of what is on your heart. People say, "Well I didn't mean it like that or what I meant to say was…" No. The Word reveals:

Matthew 12:34 KJV
"O generation of vipers, how can ye, being evil, speak good things? for out of the abundance of the heart the mouth speaketh."

Take a look at John 15:1. (Paraphrased)I am the true vine my Father is the Gardener. He cuts off every branch in Me that bares no fruit. He trims and cleans every branch that produces fruit so that it will produce even more fruit. You are already clean because of the words I have spoken to you. Remain in Me and I will remain in you. A branch cannot produce fruit alone but must remain on the vine. In the same way you cannot produce fruit alone but must remain in Me.

Remain in the Blessed Place. He is the True vine. He is the Key to the Kingdom. He is the Way, the Truth and the Light. If you don't obey Jesus you have absolutely no access to the Father. What does this say about all the prayers folks have been praying? Now, my question to you is who are you praying to? If I go to the Lord and say Lord I am asking you to bless me in this aspect or that aspect, God already knows. Prayer is communication with God. He said keep my words.

John 14:23-24 KJV
"Jesus answered and said unto him, If a man love me, he will keep my words: and my Father will love him, and we will come unto him, and make our abode with him. He that loveth me not keepeth not my sayings: and the word which ye hear is not mine, but the Father's which sent me."

The Lord is saying that He is picking and His pickings are slim. This is a harsh reality because the churches are full. You have all those who meet on the Sabbath (on Saturdays) and the rest of us who meet on Sundays. The Father is saying keep my words. He has assignments for us to fulfill and He is wondering who is going to do it. Paul said I kept the faith and I finished my course. He said I fought a good fight. So, did you keep the faith? Did you finish your course? If you didn't even start your course. When do you plan to get started?

One thing I did was promise the Lord that I would not play with His Word. I would not lie about His Word to accommodate somebody or make them feel special. That is not the will of the Father; He already informed us that seeing many will not see, hearing many will not hear. I already know when I go places it is self-evident that everybody is not going to hear.

I do realize that some will not get past the locs of my hair, the shoes that I wear or whatever the case may be to hear what God is trying to say to them. That is fine. Jesus did not come looking like the Pharisees and the Scribes; with the long robes, the veils and all that kind of stuff. He dressed just like the people of His generation. Jesus blended so well that Judas had to kiss Him in order for authorities to know who He was.

You have to ask yourself in all of my goings am I doing the will of the Father. Knowing that He is the True Vine and the Way am I really doing what He sent me here to do? Am I really being obedient to Him? It requires a lot even though He said that His yoke is easy and His burden is light. Jesus is the blessed place. There is no other place. He tells us that His word will stand forever; Heaven and earth will pass away. Giving your lives over to Him to use as He sees fit. Once that happens, He knows that there is a forever yes in your heart. He saw your heart and He knows.

Offering Strange Fire

And Nadab and Abihu died,when they offered strange fire before the Lord
Numbers 26:61

Such a tragic story… Two of the sons of Aaron offered something to God that He did not command them to do. As a result, they died. Now the interesting thing to note concerning this story is the both were being trained by their Uncle Moses. He was commanded by God to instruct them along with their father and two other brothers. Unfortunately, they decided to go and try some of the stuff out without taking into consideration the sacredness of the position.

Leviticus 10:1
And Nadab and Abihu, The sons of Aaron, took either of them his censer, and put fire therein, and put incense therein, and offered strange fire before the Lord, which He commanded them not.

They had the tools and the proper resources but one thing they did not have… they did not have the authority of the Lord. Have you moved without God's command? Have you looked at your resources and tools with the assumption of readiness yet God did not give the go ahead?

Numbers 3:3
These are the names of the sons of Aaron, the priests which were anointed, whom he consecrated to minister in the priest's office.

So not only did they have the tools but they were also anointed and consecrated. Let me bring up a very important point. Just because you are anointed, consecrated, have the resources, and tools without God's command you do not have his approval. How many times have we heard someone say they are getting ready to do something based on these things yet when asked if God told them to do it they become silent? There are also times when some will assume being anointed means I have God's approval and/or authority to move forward. Yes, I know, we have heard and seen many refer to others as being anointed for such a time as this yet they lack one thing; they do not have God's permission to act.

Right along with that we have another problem. They offered strange fire; in their haste they did something that God didn't command. Have you ever offered strange fire before God? Strange? Yes.

The things you are doing did God ask you to present them? God is so amazing that HE gave everyone their own thumbprint. Let that soak for a minute... Are you doing what GOD sent you to do or have you secretly been watching someone and decided you can do what they do? HMM! Many watch others in one form or another and then tell themselves I can do that or I can do it better. Unfortunately, GOD gives us assignments to do and while you are in mimic mode you are missing the opportunity to complete the assignment GOD actually gave you to do. You may try to duplicate what someone else is doing.... The real question for the day---Is that your assignment?

Is there a formula that can be tapped into that will
get you what God wants right away? Can you call His
name and cause your bank account to flourish? How do you look
at Him? How many prayers must be prayed? Do the prayers have to
last one hour before you can get your relationship with God on a
particular level? Maybe you say, I am not going put all that time in, do
you have a shorter version of what you do that will get me the same
results? Who shoulders do I stand on so that I can get the stuff
that He has for me? Beware... It's going take all the time He requires.

Transitioning to the New Place

"Peter, suddenly bold, said, "Master, if it's really you, call me to come to you on the water.""
Matthew   14:28   MSG

Leaving a familiar place, a place of comfort isn't always easy. Do you know the story of Joseph? It has been talked about many times throughout the years. If you know the story, then you know how Joseph ended up in Egypt. You know that his brothers sold him to his distant cousins and they walked him over to Egypt to be sold as a slave. All of a sudden, he is in a foreign land called Egypt with people he did not know.

Genesis   37:36   KJV
"And the Midianites sold him into Egypt unto Potiphar, an officer of Pharaoh's, and captain of the guard."

Now wait one minute. Who said anything about being sold? Transitioning to your *Blessed Place* does not always follow the path of comfort and ease. However, it is necessary for your development. In transition, you are embarking on something new. You're getting ready to take on a trade or a language or a culture that you never would have experienced before.

When Joseph got to Egypt he was falsely accused of raping Potiphar's wife and ended up in prison. However, in every situation, Joseph's gift always rose to the occasion. While in prison, he met the Pharaoh's butler and baker. They had dreams that Joseph interpreted. Two years later he was called on to interpret the Pharaoh's dream.

When you read the story you find out that he was forgotten. After using his gift to help others, he was forgotten. Transitioning can be a challenge in itself; so now you face the hardship of being forgotten and overlooked. Let's be honest…Who signed up for that? In addition to that, you are brought to a strange place with the expectation to grow.

Psalms 137:4 KJV
"How shall we sing the Lord's song in a strange land?"

Many times strangers are placed under scrutiny and they are not readily liked by some. It could have something to do with the fear of the unknown. Fear can grip you and keep you from getting where you need to go. On the other hand, you have a blessed place; yet, you don't bother to connect because you are too busy trying to stay comfortable. Most people like things feeling the same. Therefore, you have to change from your comfort zone.☐☐☐☐

Genesis 12:1-2 KJV
"Now the Lord had said unto Abram, Get thee out of thy country, and from thy kindred, and from thy father's house, unto a land that I will shew thee: And I will make of thee a great nation, and I will bless thee, and make thy name great; and thou shalt be a blessing:"

Abram was told to get away from three areas… He was told to leave his country, his kindred, and his father's house. Which means he had to change his surroundings. How many times have you sat down and really begin to look at the fact that God desires something more for you? Have you taken the time to find out what His desire is for you? Do you believe that there is something else that God wants to do in your life?

Exodus 14:15 KJV
"And the Lord said unto Moses, Wherefore criest thou unto me? speak unto the children of Israel, that they go forward:"

Along with embracing change, you are expected to get up and move. Sometimes we cry out… Sometimes we throw and absolute fit yet God still expects us to get up and move forward. See, sometimes when you attempt to stick with the familiar you end up missing what God had for you. That's why the Word says the Just shall live by faith. Going into the unknown will require faith.☐☐

Hebrews 11:1 KJV
"Now faith is the substance of things hoped for, the evidence of things not seen."

If you want something different then you have to embrace the unknown, the unchartered territory that God desires to give you. If you aren't careful, you'll end up dealing with the same three or four people, the same situation, the same hassle, the same fury and you wonder why you're not getting anywhere. Oftentimes, people will stay right there; calling it a place of comfort. You end up staying in misery because it is familiar. But, is the familiar your blessed place?

Now when you get where God is taking you there are somethings that will be adjusted. Lazarus was dead and wore grave clothes. However, Jesus called him out of the grave. Next he told them to loose him and set him free.

John 11:44 KJV
"And he that was dead came forth, bound hand and foot with graveclothes: and his face was bound about with a napkin. Jesus saith unto them, Loose him, and let him go."

In the case of Joseph, he got himself together, cleaned himself up, and prepared himself for greatness. As a result, he became 2nd in command. Now that's amazing! Joseph maintained regardless of what it looked like. He didn't lose his head in the process of becoming. Many times, you can find yourself in a situation like Joseph. Stay the course. Don't give up. Your day will arrive and when it does….

Will you be ready? Have you released the things that had you bound? Have you taken the time to prepare or have you been whining about the process? It's amazing that Joseph could have complained about what he had to go through but he didn't.

When a place is a blessing, you gain something from it; continually. When a place is a blessing, it's the place that you know you can trust and it is going to give you the truth regardless. A blessed place provides lessons that need to be learned. It provides teachers without you asking for one. Now ask yourself this question, if it is the blessed place for you then why did you leave? Was your assignment completed? Did you gain the things necessary to move on? Did you leave in favor of what you thought would be better. Remember, the grass looks greener on the other side.

Stay until God says go. Why? You must grow into the next season. Be careful, some people don't even know when a place is blessed or not. Their spiritual eyes are not open to it. You make connections to people with closed eyes and the next thing you know, you begin to strive.

You are not supposed to strive in your blessed place. I am not saying that the blessed place is always easy but the burden is light. In other words, you can handle it without falling apart. If you talk to people often enough they will tell you, "I'm just doing what I got to do; I'm doing me." "I'm trying to survive." That is not a blessed place. A lot of times, when you ask folks they'll tell you, "I really don't like it but this is the going thing right now." If they knew another place to go, they would go but how do you get there? "Who's going to open the door for me?" They will wait for a door opener. Sometimes you don't realize some of the stuff you have been through is actually your door opener. God has given you a ticket to go to the unknown. It requires faith.

Joseph did nothing to them but they did something to him. Now he is the one to help them get the resources they need to survive. It is funny how the one you offend, may be the one you need to help you get to the next level.

That's why it is so important not to burn any bridges. You never know if you going to have to cross that bridge again; when all else is forgotten. We'll throw people away in a minute. Don't throw them away; you may need them. I like to tell people that God is the Creator, if you didn't create anything; don't throw anything away. You never know when that might be the one that can give you a job; when everybody closed their eyes to you. They may be the one that opens up their home to you; while everybody else forsakes you.

Every Good Gift

"Every good gift and every perfect gift is from above, and cometh down from the Father of lights, with whom is no variableness, neither shadow of turning."
James 1:17 KJV

Have you ever thought about why God created you? Why He put you here? You know I used to ask myself that same question, "God why am I here? Why did you put me on this earth?" When you begin to realize that you are supposed to be here and you were not a mistake.
Your parents didn't slip up and have you. Even if you were a mistake to them, you were not a mistake to God. It does not matter if they were married or not, God said in His Word that children are a gift from Him. When you realize that you are a gift to this world; you will start looking at your life differently. Not only are you a gift, you are gifted.

When Joseph came up before the Pharaoh, the Pharaoh didn't look at him saying, "Wait a minute; were you in my prison system all this time? No, I don't want anybody from prison. I can't do that." He trusted a former prisoner. Pharaoh had no reason to trust Joseph's word. Pharaoh didn't even mention it. He told him what the issue was; I had this dream and it troubles me. Joseph explained it. Before you knew it, Joseph was 2nd in command. How does that work? You go from being last on the list to be the one that is in charge.

One thing about gifts, they can't be hidden. You can attempt to hide them but at some point, they will show up. In other words, if you are a leader no matter what situation you find yourself in, your leadership will show up. If you are a singer, you will get around other people singing and all of a sudden you sing you weren't trying to be boisterous or throw yourself out there but suddenly, you are leading the pact. People began to wonder how you got that position. You tell them, you don't know. What happened is simple. Your gift made room for you; it was your gift. You're reaping the benefits of the gift; you didn't force it.

Proverbs 18:16 KJV
"A man's gift maketh room for him, and bringeth him before great men."

Many times your view point about your gifts comes from where you've been. Based on that you figure, well if these people think that I'm a certain way then everybody thinks that. You then resolve to saying, "I'm not going to bother." You know what happens to a lot of youngsters who feel this way? They refuse to go to college because somebody told them they weren't smart enough. Then they spread these negative words around somebody who's a total stranger "Well bless your heart, are you going to school?" Who encourages them to do it? You need a couple of good strangers in your life to give you some validity on the situation. Some of those folks that know you are not going to tell you the truth. It's unfortunate. We all have family that will not tell us the truth. I don't care how much you've been cooking that cake, they will tell you it is too dry or too wet; they will never tell you it is good. They will continue to say, "I didn't really like it, it didn't taste all that hot.

Joseph didn't walk into the house and say, "Hey, I'm a leader, put me in charge. I'll do it for you." Potiphar watched Joseph from a distance and noticed something about him. Funny, when you're around your own kin folk, some of the folks you know; they don't seem to notice too much of anything.

You're just the same old, same old, "Aw yeah well you know that's how she is; that's how he is, that's how this is." On the other hand, you find some people who are not accustomed to you so they have to watch you. They are looking; they listen to you when you speak and they watch how you carry yourself. The people who knew you from way back when try to pinpoint who you are based solely on your past; the stranger doesn't have your past to go on, so they have to look at you for who you are today.

As in Joseph's story the stranger puts you to work. It's business… They take your gift seriously. Meanwhile you have been sitting there thinking that you are less than. You know some tend to do this? They say this all the time. Some go where they are tolerated while the celebrated place remains dormant; they continue to stand with folks that put up with them until they get what they want. However, when you go where you are celebrated you will feel better about yourself; more than you ever have before. All of a sudden, you begin to enjoy being around others; the one who celebrates you. They make you feel like you are somebody. You feel like, you could really do something with yourself and that you are not just wasting time sitting around. God did not create you and bring you here without purpose.

Go where you are appreciated and valued. The place God designed for you. Those that cover you and pray for you.

Person, Place, and Thing

Sometimes your blessed place is more than a place. Actually it can include a person, place and/or thing. That person maybe the one to help propel you to where you need to go or talk you into something that you wouldn't have trusted or believed about yourself. They see what you can't... Samuel saw what Saul couldn't see. Saul was looking for the lost animals of his father yet God had so much more in store for His life.

1 Samuel 9:15-17 KJV
"Now the Lord had told Samuel in his ear a day before Saul came, saying, To morrow about this time I will send thee a man out of the land of Benjamin, and thou shalt anoint him to be captain over my people Israel, that he may save my people out of the hand of the Philistines: for I have looked upon my people, because their cry is come unto me. And when Samuel saw Saul, the Lord said unto him, Behold the man whom I spake to thee of! this same shall reign over my people."

Samuel was told to prepare for Saul's arrival. Saul had no clue. This should dispel the myth concerning prophecy. Every time God speaks will not lend itself to ongoing confirmation. In other words, do not allow yourself to get caught up in the twisted reality that has captivated the minds of so many trying to be relevant.

Often God speaks and the directives are foreign in terms of His selection and strategy. Another thing to ponder, it will seem like an overnight success to others; it is not. It's just that everything you've been through over time has prepared you for this moment. During the time of isolation, many paid no attention to you so when you go forth it will seem as if it was overnight. Look at artists who sing. It looks like they've created their album or big hit today, but what you don't see are the years that they struggled to get to that point. It just seemed so easy.

Matthew 11:28-30 KJV
"Come unto me, all ye that labour and are heavy laden, and I will give you rest. Take my yoke upon you, and learn of me; for I am meek and lowly in heart: and ye shall find rest unto your souls. For my yoke is easy, and my burden is light."

His yoke is easy and his burden is light. Life has its bumps and curves; however God's yoke is easy. The yoke fits around your neck to guide and identify you as belonging to someone. Some have taken on the yokes of others and wonder why they are having a hard time getting free.

Getting back to Joseph... Through the entire ordeal we can clearly see that Joseph is not the same little brother anymore. He has been exposed to other stuff. He is fully integrated into another culture. Joseph has changed. See, people tell others they can't change; yes, you can; you need to pay attention to God's instructions and when He brings opportunity you have to act on it unless He told you otherwise.

Joshua 3:3-4 KJV
"And they commanded the people, saying, When ye see the ark of the covenant of the Lord your God, and the priests the Levites bearing it, then ye shall remove from your place, and go after it. Yet there shall be a space between you and it, about two thousand cubits by measure: come not near unto it, that ye may know the way by which ye must go: for ye have not passed this way heretofore."

When you get to *The Blessed Place* stay right there. Before you know it, you're wondering how those doors opened up for you. Opportunity after opportunity continues to show up at your doorstep. They are not going to open in some of those little areas you were hoping they were going to open in. You have to go where God is sending you. Then you have to stay there long enough for Him to help. You are going to have to listen to who God has chosen to assist you.

You know you are about to go somewhere because that person is not scared of any of the systems. They pray for you without hesitation because they know God is taking you somewhere. In other words, they will help you walk you to it. Now, you are walking together. You have somebody who has the inside track. They have some contacts with folks that you normally wouldn't consider them having. They will nourish you. You will began to learn things in the weirdest of ways. You end up in a place where your whole life becomes study time. Education is yours whether it's formal or informal. They are constantly trying to get you information. They are trying to help you get where you need to go. That's a Blessed Place. Are you in your Blessed Place? It is something to think about.

Are you standing in your Blessed Place? Or are you standing outside of it? Do you see it? Maybe you tip your toe into it every now and then; but you won't go ahead and get submerged by that thing. How many of us know what we have to do to get ahead but are not willing to do it? It might be because of fear. This is why in Genesis chapter 46:3, God said, "And he said, I am God, the God of thy father: fear not to go down into Egypt; for I will there make of thee a great nation."(KJV)

He said go down into Egypt. That means you will have to do some traveling. You will have to do some moving and changing to get where you need to go. The time has come for you to finally get to the place where you realize you are here for a reason. You are not here by accident. You were created with a purpose. You are destined to be here.

It is at this point you will seek out your blessed place. You will know it when you get there because you won't feel comfortable or settled. In fact you might almost be mad. You might get mad with the people who pushed you to your blessed place. You might catch an attitude and say, "I'm going home." What you fail to realize is those people, that place and that torn up feeling; is exactly where you need to be connected. Why? Because that place won't allow you to stay the way you are. It will force you to be something that you didn't think you could ever be. Those weird things will force you to face the dreams you put on the back burner.

That's right... I say this often and I will say it again. Many people place their dreams on the back burner. You have goals on the back burner. You have all kinds of visions on hold. Do you write, sing or draw? So many of us can do some of these things, but that is the stuff on the back burner; thinking other people won't like it. More than likely, it was in the wrong hands and you were with the wrong people. See I can write some stuff and pass it to you. You might say, "Oh that's cute" and keep it moving. But then if it is put in the right hands, all of a sudden it becomes a job. Now, someone is willing to pay me to write for someone else. All of a sudden, you see my name on somebody else's CD. You see my name in the newspaper.

All this can happen when you put your talent in the right hands. If you don't remember anything else that I have in this book, you must check the place that you are standing in. Who are you surrounding yourself with? You have to be truthful with yourself as to whether or not that place is blessed. If you are not growing; it is not a blessed place. It's killing you. It's not helping you and it's not going to get you where you need to go. Unless you have refused to grow which is a bird of a different feather.

Remember this, many people are supposed to be in college. Many are supposed to own businesses. I am not saying this to be cute; it is real. God did not make you the last on the list. We tend to give up too easily. We say, "Oh it's not going to work out." So, we give up. We will say, "They don't like me no way" and we give up. We will say, "I'm not going over there to do all of that" and we give up.

Sometimes we are so scared to go because of the unknown. Everything is new. The surroundings are foreign. You may say, "This is weird to me; I'm not familiar with it". So out of fear we don't go. Don't allow fear to hold you up or hold you back. Don't allow fear to keep you from moving ahead! It is time to go to your blessed place. When you get to your blessed place, you will know it. There is a level of seriousness that hits you. You won't let nothing or nobody keep you from getting there. Once you've arrived STAY PUT!

Reality Check

The Blessed Place is so much more than identifying yourself as a Christian or going to church every week. Believe it or not some actually think that all they have to do is blink at the Word. You've probably heard some of the excuses such as: I don't have to do what everybody else is doing, it doesn't take all that, I can get in just the way I am with no changes etc... Have you used any of these yourself?

So now, we have a variety of people believing that they are in *The Blessed Place* because they said so yet won't read any further than the verses of scripture that promises He is going to prepare a place for us. And if He goes to prepare a place for us, He is coming back to get us.

John 14:2-3 KJV
"In my Father's house are many mansions: if it were not so, I would have told you. I go to prepare a place for you. And if I go and prepare a place for you, I will come again, and receive you unto myself; that where I am, there ye may be also."

He is telling us all this beautiful stuff, but we won't read the first part or go any further. Thomas said to Jesus, "Lord we don't know where you're going so how can we know the way." Jesus said you know the way to the place where I am going. How can Jesus say you already know when one of His boys is saying, no I don't know where you're going? How can you walk with someone and He says you got it but you say no I don't have it. Jesus answered saying, (and this is something we love to quote)

35

John 14:4-10 KJV
"And whither I go ye know, and the way ye know. Thomas saith unto him,
Lord, we know not whither thou goest; and how can we know the way? Jesus
saith unto him, I am the way, the truth, and the life: no man cometh unto the
Father, but by me. If ye had known me, ye should have known my Father also:
and from henceforth ye know him, and have seen him. Philip saith unto him,
Lord, shew us the Father, and it sufficeth us. Jesus saith unto him, Have I been
so long time with you, and yet hast thou not known me, Philip? he that hath
seen me hath seen the Father; and how sayest thou then, Shew us the Father?
Believest thou not that I am in the Father, and the Father in me? the words that
I speak unto you I speak not of myself: but the Father that dwelleth in me, he
doeth the works."

"I am the Way, the Truth and the Light; the only way to the Father is through Me." How can you walk with the Way and not know that He is the Way? Because, seeing you still don't see and hearing you still don't hear. And that is what He kept saying to His disciples. That is why He taught worship to a harlot. He taught her right at a place she would be familiar with; an ancient landmark, Jacob's Well. She was faithful to that Well until Jesus came and showed her a more excellent way. He shifted her, because she was already attentive to the place that God had ordained for the Samaritans up until that point. Too many people will sit there and avoid the landmark trying to get somewhere else. You have not even occupied the first seat that God put you in. You keep wondering where the next place is, but you have to occupy through the place of obedience. If you are not obedient to God, He is telling you through His Word, you really don't love me.

People will fix all this other stuff and hope that God will be pleased in the Kingdom. Many will go and say to themselves, let me just brush up on God right quick and get my quick fix by going to church a couple Sundays in a row. Now you know how it is. Folks will come to church and get a shout in and feel like that is what is going to cover them for the week, for the month, or for the year. They figure they don't have to sit or remain in the Blessed Place. All they have to do is just look at the inside of a church building every now and then. What happened to being developed? What happened to growing in God?

The Father says no you might do that on the Earth, but that is not how I work in My Kingdom. The end result is, you have a disciple that doesn't even know that he is walking with the Way; the whole time. But all he has been doing is churching it. He has been eating dinner with Him, going by His house, spending time with Him, praying with Him and all this stuff yet he still does not know who He really is. But a harlot can get into place quickly. Something that has taken many a few years to do she got it in minutes. I am the Way, the Truth, the Light and the only way to the Father is through Me. If you really knew Me, you would know My Father too.

John 14:12 KJV
"Verily, verily, I say unto you, He that believeth on me, the works that I do shall he do also; and greater works than these shall he do; because I go unto my Father."

He is talking naturally, supernaturally and He is trying to tell them; I am standing right here. I have been standing here the whole time. I have not been closed off to you. I have opened Myself up to you. Truth is not withheld from us. God is saying I made sure to put it out there. Then Philip says, "Lord, show us the Father; that is all we need." So even after Jesus kept telling them, "I'm standing right here" he still didn't know. He still did not know what was going on. Too many people are running around here saying the same thing; I feel the presence of God. No you felt the presence of the one sitting next to you. You felt an emotional kick; you had a quick fix.

You really did not feel the presence of God. Folks like to believe that obedience and His presence are not connected. But the Bible says in John four that God is a Spirit and they that worship Him must worship Him in spirit and truth. If you don't walk in truth, how can you walk in worship? If you don't walk in obedience then how can you walk in worship? That's impossible; because Jesus said that you have to obey him. Jesus said that I am the Way and you can't get to the Father unless you come through Him. So if you don't obey the words of Jesus, then you have not gotten through to the Father. This means you are still at the surface level, struggling to get past Jesus.

Some people have forgotten what happened in the Garden of Eden. There was an angel with a sword. When Adam and Eve were released from the Garden, they could not go back. Now, just like Adam and Eve could not re-enter the Garden unless they go past the angel; you cannot get to God without going through Jesus. This is where He wants His people to return to Him. Through Jesus. Why? He is the Blessed Place. This is the purpose of Psalms 91, where He says I will hide you under the shadow of My wings. That's where you find your protection, your rest, your comfort and all of that good stuff. But in order to get there under the shadow of His wings, you have to go through Jesus. What Jesus is saying is if anybody hears My words and obey Me you have access to My Father. His words have already attracted you enough to cause you to say Yes, Jesus; but if you want to come any closer you will have to obey Me.

Then He will reveal His real self to you. Just like He did for the harlot at the well. Many want Him to reveal Himself; they want the revelation. Give me the logos and the Rhema I want it all. However, the Lord says, okay I've been giving you the logos, but hearing you still don't hear. I'm trying to talk to you, you keep reading and it is right there staring at you.

John   14:8-9 KJV
"Philip saith unto him, Lord, shew us the Father, and it sufficeth us. Jesus saith unto him, Have I been so long time with you, and yet hast thou not known me, Philip? he that hath seen me hath seen the Father; and how sayest thou then, Shew us the Father?

Philip says, Lord show us the Father that's all we need. Jesus answered and said I've been with you a long time now, do you still not know me; Philip? Whoever has seen Me has seen the Father so why do you say show us the Father? Don't you believe that I am in the Father and the Father lives in Me? Well, Phillip believed because of the miracles that I have done.

When you figure out that He's the only way to the Father you will realize that many who call themselves followers of Jesus need a reality check.

Remember what John told us in John 1:1, In the beginning was
the Word and the Word was with God and
the Word was God. He goes on to tell us in verse
14 that the Word became flesh and dwelt among men. The Word
that you are eating and reading is the Father. Then He tells us, I tell you
the truth whoever believes in Me will do the same things that I do.

John 1:14 KJV
"And the Word was made flesh, and dwelt among us, (and we beheld his glory,
the glory as of the only begotten of the Father,) full of grace and truth."

We are not even talking about the greater stuff yet. We're talking about
the same things that Jesus did. In other words, Peter should have been
accused of hanging with Jesus. When you hang with Jesus you start
acting like Him. There are parts of His character that will be hard to
miss. People will say wait a minute you look like
Jesus. You know people get really excited when they are out around
town and someone says to them, "Are you a minister?" Or they tell
others, "I am a minister." Yea okay but that still does not mean you act
like Jesus. Okay let's just get real. We know some "Christians". That
word "Christian", the more I hear it, the more I wonder if people really
understand what it means. □

Walking In His Shoes

*"So keep the commands of the Lord your God by walking in His ways and
fearing Him."*
Deuteronomy 8:6 HCSB

Ask yourself, when you look in the mirror who do you see? Are you
unstable? The Word of God says that a double minded man is unstable
in all of his ways. The Father is not going to try to occupy an unstable
vessel. That's why He told Peter when you are converted then go
strengthen your brother. In other words, when you give your all to me
then I'm going to shine through you; then you can go and
help everybody else. But I can't get you to everybody else until I am
with you. I need you and me to be on the same ticket. That is a part of
your blessed place. The mirror, the Word of God. Every time you read
a scripture; that is where class begins for you. The Bible is supposed to
be your class room.

One of the things about Jesus, His classes took place all the time. It did
not matter where He was. His class room was wherever He wanted His
class room to be; whether His class was on the mountain top or in the
valley. He did things this way so we would know how to do them.

Matthew 11:1 KJV
*"And it came to pass, when Jesus had made an end of commanding his twelve
disciples, he departed thence to teach and to preach in their cities."*

He taught in their cities… That means He entered their cities to assist with ministry. There was work that needed to be done and He didn't mind doing it. What are you doing? After receiving instructions do you head out to get it done?

Let me throw this question in. Why did you get saved? Did you count the cost? Being saved means you've just shifted. I know this may be hard for some because they thought growing up in church gave leverage. Why? Because in church it felt good to tell somebody I been saved for twenty years or thirty years, but if you really admit it how many of those years really belonged to the Lord? What part of that showed singleness with the Father? How many of those years were spent complaining? I know I'm not the only one…

The Word of God tells us that Jesus never said a mumbling word. He did not say "Now, why you doing this to me? Look how you stabbed me in my hands. Ouch! Why did you pierce me in my side? Why y'all throwing them stones? Why did y'all beat me like you did? You made me carry that Cross." He did not say a mumbling word. His Words was Father forgive them. When He walked through the streets and kept on walking; there was forgiveness everywhere; love pouring out. Even when they called Simon forward to help him carry that part of the Cross. He did not say "Simon, Lift that up just a little bit, so that I can catch that soldier (hit him) right over there or trip this soldier right over here." He did not try and take His foot and see if He could drag it and knock somebody down. He did not say "look I know I said I was going to walk this thing in the flesh but I need to roll up My divinity sleeves and cut a few butts just a little bit because I know the devil out here somewhere. I need to mess with a few people."

You know if it was any of us who had that power and was in that spot, we would have been acting like X-Men, super-friends, the avengers; you know what I'm talking about. I would have been acting like Storm from X-Men all day. I would have been sitting there turning to the side and all kinds of dark clouds would have been on the scene. You can't mess with the girl; don't even try it. I would have said "Mary, you hungry?

But see, the Lord God said that He looked through all of these generations and He could not find one good enough to walk in the shoes Jesus filled. We got this thing backwards. Church folks like to believe that they are the sweetest thing since slide bread. They are the ones that are really doing it for the Father.

It is almost sarcastic; if you will. Like you don't know that by now? It is kind of like Philip and Thomas asking all these questions and the Father is standing right here. I am the way. I am your blessed place. I am standing right here. What else do you want? So when it all comes down to it their excuses held no water with the Father. I try to tell folks you are wasting your time going back and forth, over and over again when you have no desire to shift. The church is not supposed to be for us to come together just to look at each other, go home and say that I have done my due for the day. When the Father is waiting for folks to start doing what He did. It does not mean you get in there and leave.

Now you are hitting the road and going out to start seeking out people who you can help. Jesus did His work according to order. When He started out, He made sure John the Baptist baptized Him. He did not by pass the way of doing things. Why? He wanted His people to follow suit. If you are going to be a leader, we will know by the way that you follow. If you sit there and half step while you follow you are telling us already how your leadership will look. How many will admit, I didn't do right as a follower but I expect for folks to do right while I am leading.

True believers of God bare Jesus Christ through their obedience. If you are not obeying Him then you have to face your truth today. Obedience is what shows Heaven that you Love the Father. Check your obedience by writing a list of the things He has told you to do; an honest list. Then ask yourself the question; did I really do these things? Or did I have excuses for not doing them? If you had an excuse it does not count. If you did not do it; it does not count.

My Father loves those who love me; those who keep His commands. When people walk around talking about God is love and that God loves me so much.

The question is do you do what Jesus tells you to do. If you say, "No I don't do everything He tells me to do." Well then, be free to read John 14. There are a lot of folks who have crossed out half of the Bible. They say that the Old Testament is not to be followed. They say that Paul was just another writer. Then I tell them that you don't know Jesus very well. If you know my Daddy in the flesh, you would know that He is the hardest one of them all. He said I did not come with peace I came with a sword. Now, Moses did not say that, Paul did not say that, it was Jesus Himself; the same One who turned to Peter and said we don't fight like that. He said I came with a sword. Most people would think that He is talking about a natural sword but He is actually talking about the Word of God. He said, Look I don't need the physical sword. My Word is sharper than any two edged sword and it cuts better. It cuts with precision. You cannot get any more precise then the way that He cuts. So, where do you stand? Jesus says it again; here comes another disciple in John 14:22 asking the Lord when do You plan to show Yourself to us and not to the rest of the world. Jesus answers again saying, if you love Me, you will obey My teachings. Jesus keeps breaking it down for people. Jesus is simply saying over and over, if people love Me they will obey My teachings. In turn, My Father will love them; we will come to them and make Our home with them.

We must face facts...This is true for grown children. Well. For example: If your mama is the one who has the relationship with God and you move out; you will know the difference. You will know. Sometimes children grow up under an anointed mommy and daddy who were doing things for the Lord. When the children move away, they wondering what happened to the peace and the anointing. That is why you must understand it is your relationship with God that brings His presence. Where do you stand?

Lot moved away from Abram and all of a sudden all hell broke loose. It was not all bushy tail love for the Father anymore. Why? He was sheltered by the anointing of another. He was sheltered by the intimate connection of another. Love for Jesus requires obedience and obedience is better than sacrifice.

This is the Word of God. Jesus also said, disobedience is as witchcraft, this is one reason why we see so much witch craft in the church. In God's eye sight they are one in the same. In the Body of Christ we see so much of that. This is why ministries get shut down, why relationships get all messed up, and why leaders fall. It is because of the disobedience. We don't want to read these little things that are clearly written in the Word of God. The Blessed Place was not the place that people change at any given time, the blessed place is in God. And a lot of people want to believe yeah, I'm in God. You can't tell me I'm not in God but oh yes we can because according to the word it is quite simple. The Lord put this stuff in The Word; His criteria.

Jesus doesn't hold anybody back from being a part of His crew. Folks have watered down this whole Jesus thing into this nice little He'll let anybody in. It is true but you have to obey. He doesn't care if you are white, black, blue, green, or purple. He doesn't care if you are male or female. You could have been out in the streets two seconds ago. He doesn't care; come on. The only thing is when you get over here He does expect you to shift; He does expect you to obey Him.

Your Blessed Forecast

"Be careful to obey all the commands I am giving you today. Then you will live and multiply, and you will enter and occupy the land the Lord swore to give your ancestors."
Deuteronomy 8:1 NLT

This passage holds key information on moving from where you are to where you need to be. The first part says to be careful to obey. The Word careful signifies that you must be alert, sensible, and deliberate. So when you think of being careful to obey, you must take the time to pay attention as you journey through life. There's no time to wander or attempt to do things without thoughtful consideration. God intends for His people to take His instructions seriously. How can you take them seriously if you don't read and meditate on them daily?

Psalms 1:1-2 KJV
"Blessed is the man that walketh not in the counsel of the ungodly, nor standeth in the way of sinners, nor sitteth in the seat of the scornful. But his delight is in the law of the Lord; and in his law doth he meditate day and night."

Then He said you will live and multiply. How can you really live separated from the Word of God? This is the time to take a stand and refuse to let anything get in the way of developing a real relationship with Him.

Romans 8:35-39 KJV
"Who shall separate us from the love of Christ? shall tribulation, or distress, or persecution, or famine, or nakedness, or peril, or sword? As it is written, For thy sake we are killed all the day long; we are accounted as sheep for the slaughter. Nay, in all these things we are more than conquerors through him that loved us. For I am persuaded, that neither death, nor life, nor angels, nor principalities, nor powers, nor things present, nor things to come, Nor height, nor depth, nor any other creature, shall be able to separate us from the love of God, which is in Christ Jesus our Lord."

GOD is doing a new thing...let go of the STUFF that keeps you from being GREAT! This is the word that God gave me. Remember how He told Joseph there was going to be seven years of famine and seven years of feast? Many are missing their blessed place because the famine hit in some area of their life.

Genesis 41:56-57 KJV
"And the famine was over all the face of the earth: And Joseph opened all the storehouses, and sold unto the Egyptians; and the famine waxed sore in the land of Egypt. And all countries came into Egypt to Joseph for to buy corn; because that the famine was so sore in all lands."

Be careful that you don't close your eyes to Your Blessed Place because it doesn't look the way you had anticipated. Also pay attention in this season to the advice you receive. The wrong advice can set you back years. On the other hand, there is safety in the multitude of godly counsel.

Isaiah 30:1-2 KJV
"Woe to the rebellious children, saith the Lord, that take counsel, but not of me; and that cover with a covering, but not of my spirit, that they may add sin to sin: That walk to go down into Egypt, and have not asked at my mouth; to strengthen themselves in the strength of Pharaoh, and to trust in the shadow of Egypt!"

Do take note, Joseph remained in Egypt and prospered there. It did not say we would do the same. We must ask God His will for our lives. God considers counsel to be valuable. Consequently, it must come from the place He authorized.

This season is unique; as a result, many people are leaving the blessed place to go to other places. Don't confuse the times. They begin to see that when they are over here it happens, but if I go over there it does not. This is a strong indication of your need to get back in the flow. Joseph said God sent me before you to preserve a posterity for you in the earth. These blessings were to save your lives by a great deliverance. Joseph said to his brothers, it was not you that sent me here; it was God. He has made Pharaoh a father to me and lord of his entire house.

As we end the third book of *The Blessed Place Series*, I want to share with you the Forecast. What is a Forecast…to make a statement about what is likely to happen, usually relating to the Weather, Business, and the Economy. It's not going to come together the way you thought it would. Actually it will supersede every thought you've had for God's thoughts and ways are higher.

Isaiah 55:9 KJV
"For as the heavens are higher than the earth, so are my ways higher than your ways, and my thoughts than your thoughts."

Just as the heavens are higher than the earth, God's ways and thoughts are higher. Who should you trust to lead you? That is enough to have a Blessed Forecast! We are told not to lean to our own understanding. The Father has some stuff working on your behalf that you don't know about.

Isaiah 65:24 KJV
"And it shall come to pass, that before they call, I will answer; and while they are yet speaking, I will hear."

Did you read that? He says that He will answer BEFORE you call. Absolutely amazing…that's the kind of God we serve. He knows the issues we face before we face them. He directs our steps; He leads us.

Joseph understood. He realized that God sent him to Egypt. Joseph said to his brothers, "⁵ Now therefore be not grieved, nor angry with yourselves, that ye sold me hither: for God did send me before you to preserve life."Genesis 45:5(KJV)

That statement required some strength from God. It
requires spending so much time with God that He has melded His character into you to the point that you are able to complete your mission knowing He is with you. Now you're able to stand there giving a word of encouragement without a second thought. That takes God! How else could you stand there and love anyone unless you have given your heart over to God. God had to provide healing over the years. Through the years the gifts and blessing of the
Lord continued to show up. Regardless of the circumstances you face in life God created you to prosper;

Your gift will cause you to prosper. For example; certain trees cannot grow everywhere. The trees may need a special climate to prosper. They need the weather to be a certain way. If you tried to grow them in places where the weather was not appropriate; you will know it because something will be wrong with that tree. Just like that tree, your gift won't feel right out of place.

You will learn that some places or people; you just can't go around. Your gift does fine in some places but try to plant yourself where the climate is not right; your gift will not flow. There are even some family members that you cannot be around.

Mark 6:4-6 KJV
"But Jesus said unto them, A prophet is not without honour, but in his own country, and among his own kin, and in his own house. And he could there do no mighty work, save that he laid his hands upon a few sick folk, and healed them. And he marvelled because of their unbelief. And he went round about the villages, teaching."

☐

Jesus understood this. When it comes to your gift all you can say is, "Hey, how you doing now?" or "Hey what's going on?" Then you have to keep moving. Many times for the sake of the relationship, people will try to force the tree to grow in the midst of the cold people; hoping that they'll accept them. Hoping they will accept the fruit and then finally you will be in this happy go lucky kind of situation. Soon you find out it is not going to work. Hence the importance of knowing and having a blessed place. You have got to know what your blessed place is.

You have to ask yourself the question… Is this my Blessed Place? The same folks that I've been looking at, are they a part of my Blessed Place? You know as I stated earlier a Blessed Place is a place of growth. You have to ask yourself "am I growing?"

You need to ask yourself the question what God wants to do with my life. I truly do not believe that God has left man on this earth to try to work just to get enough to get by; to live on a few dollars here and there. I just don't believe that's what God considers a Blessed Place. Yes, sometimes you do have to go through some stuff. It does not always feel good. You don't like it! Most people don't like when folks say things about them. But some of that stuff is going to force you into the place you need to go.

Sometimes we don't like to face reality. Could the real problem be you? For example, it is funny how people do not respect others, but they want respect? We don't love folks like we need to but we want folks to love us. We want the things sometimes that we're not willing to put out. It's time for real change. What can you do right now that will shift your current position to the place God designed?

Some people are going to be hated as this season progresses because it requires certain elements that some will have and others will not. Don't miss out and yet be so close to it. It is kind of like Moses; some will see the Promised Land but can't go in. You know how you hear people say, "I can taste it, but I just can't put my hands on it." Don't let this be you. Learn, grow, and mature into the person

God desires and RUN to HIM! Stay right there and don't move! For then you will be in your blessed place!

As a Kingdom Leadership Trainer, Certified Life Transformational Coach, Biblical Therapist, and Apostle, **Tracey** continues to empower her clients to overcome personal obstacles while improving their relationships in family, business, and ministry; she assists them in finding their voice and using it to achieve their own goals.

With over 35+ years in ministry, **Tracey** speaks regularly to church congregations, ministerial leaders, business staff and management about resolving conflict issues and other matters pertaining to healthy connections. She has continued to seek the Lord for guidance in instructing, motivating, and empowering His Leaders to Soar. One of the ways God led her to accomplish that was through T.G.A.P Systems LLC. This includes:

- The Core Outreach Network
- The Core Training Institute
- TGAP Consultants
- EmPOWERment University
- Ministry In The Know

Tracey has been included as an author in several anthologies entitled "This Far by Faith" and "Dear Daddy". Along with her books "The Blessed Place", "The Blessed Place Workbook", "When God Speaks: Discovering Your Power in Prayer", **Tracey** recently completed her fourth book, "SHH! God is Speaking! Can you hear Him?", When she's not writing, coaching or counseling, she continues to travel throughout the US and abroad sharing the word. If you would like more information feel free to contact **Tracey** using one of the following methods:

Ministry In The Know
TraceytheCoach@gmail.com

On FaceBook use
@TraceytheCoach

On Twitter use
@ApostleTraceyG